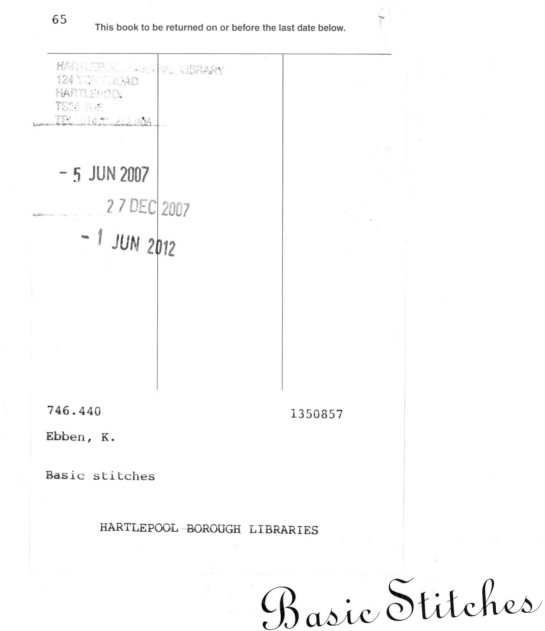

Basic Stitches

Basic Stitches

Katie Ebben

PHOTOGRAPHY BY CHRIS TUBBS

First published in 2006 by Conran Octopus Limited
a part of Octopus Publishing Group
2–4 Heron Quays, London E14 4JP
www.conran-octopus.co.uk

British Library Cataloguing-in-Publication Data.
A catalogue record for this book is available from the British Library.

ISBN 1 84091 424 6
Printed in China

Publishing Director: Lorraine Dickey
Art Directors: Lucy Gowans and Jonathan Christie
Executive Editor: Zia Mattocks
Designer: Nicky Barneby
Editor: Emma Clegg
Illustrator: Alice Tait
Stylist: Katie Ebben
Photographer's Assistant: Natasha Sturny
Production Manager: Angela Couchman

Contents

Introduction

I come from a long line of stitchers on both my maternal and paternal side. My sideboard and various suitcases in the attic are stuffed to bursting with the prodigious output of my female ancestors. I vaguely remember Big Granny (who was actually very small but a great-grandmother and hence the name) stitching an enormous patchwork quilt and dainty tea cosy in the most glorious flower-power fabrics of the 1970s for my parents. Both still make the odd appearance on beds and, of course, the teapot from time to time. Alongside this are all the ultra-delicate cutwork tablecloths whose fine edges and borders look like lace. I can't begin to imagine how long they took to make or how anyone had the patience or the eyesight to complete them. These pieces of embroidery have become family heirlooms — items that are cherished and still used to decorate bedside tables or to make teatime special on Christmas Day.

Like many people, I was taught to sew by my mother. Because I am left handed and she is right handed, she had the added headache of trying to teach me how to do everything back to front. I found knitting, which she also taught me, harder to grasp and so I graduated to the sewing machine fairly quickly. While my mother is a painstaking perfectionist, I prefer instant results and tend towards a 'who needs to follow a pattern?' philosophy. This is one of the reasons I trained as a textile designer, because I found creating individual pieces so much more rewarding. Although I worked with printed textiles, both machine and hand embroidery featured prominently in my work, giving it that extra element of embellishment and depth.

While making the projects for this book, I joined some friends who had decided to set up a Craft Night, the idea being that we all liked making things and it is more fun doing it in good company. We probably do more talking than crafting, and yet it is great to have creative input from people who can teach you new techniques or give you guidance when you get stuck. One of the most amusing aspects of Craft Night was the speed at which a set of (almost) unspoken rules fell into place: the food on offer is either risotto or baked potatoes and pudding is always of the school-dinner variety; and no mending is allowed unless you are the host or you are between major projects and awaiting creative inspiration.

If your hand sewing to date extends only to the mending-when-necessary variety, such as sewing on buttons or doing a quick repair on a split seam, then you have all the basic skills required to make every project in this book. Start at the beginning with the easiest one and build your way up from there. If you are nervous and feel the need for more guidance, then why not set up your own Craft Night and get your friends to bring their own friends along so you can meet new people at the same time.

Happy stitchin'!

Cross Stitch

Cross Stitch

Cross stitch is one of the oldest and most widely used embroidery stitches, and its use can be traced as far back as Ancient Egypt. The peoples of the Greek islands, Turkey, Romania, Austria, Sweden, Norway and Denmark all used cross stitch as the main stitch for their traditional embroidery. You will also have seen cross stitch on samplers and its alternative name is sample stitch. It is mostly used for filling, outlining, creating borders and motifs. Once you've picked up the method for cross stitch it is a very easy and rhythmic stitch, making it a good one to do if you need a little calming down – a kind of stitcher's meditation.

How To Do It

There are two ways of doing cross stitch: you can either complete one stitch before starting on the next or work half of each stitch for an entire row before returning along the row to finish the second part of each stitch. A right-handed stitcher will find it easiest to work from right to left and a left-handed stitcher will prefer working from left to right.

Always keep your cross stitches evenly spaced and at the same height and width. If this proves difficult you can use a water-based fabric pen to draw a parallel line as a guide for the stitches, or alternatively you can count the threads on the fabric you are sewing.

SINGLE CROSS STITCH To make one complete stitch bring the needle up at A and then down at B – this will form one half of the cross. To make the second part bring the needle up through the fabric at C and back down at D.

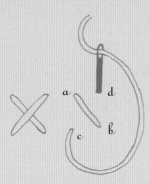

LINES OF CROSS STITCH Starting on the bottom right-hand side of your fabric (if you are left handed start from the bottom left), bring the needle up through the fabric at A and down at B to create a slanting stitch. To begin the next stitch bring the needle up through the fabric at C. Continue repeating these steps until you have filled an entire row.

To complete the stitch, reverse the direction so that you are working from left to right (or right to left if you are left handed) and cross over each stitch previously made by taking the needle down through the fabric at D and back up through the fabric at E. Repeat the sequence until the row is completed.

Creating Your Own Designs

You can easily adapt drawings or your own designs into cross-stitch patterns. Simply trace the design onto tracing paper using a pencil and transfer this onto graph paper. Then, using a pen, fill in the gridline nearest to the freehand drawing outline so that you are left with a motif that has only horizontal and vertical lines. Each square on the graph paper represents a cross stitch. The size of square on your graph paper will determine the size of your stitches, so use larger-format paper if you are a beginner to make the process easier and quicker.

To transfer the design you will need to count the threads in your fabric – for example one cross stitch might measure four threads across and four threads up. You can use either loose-weave fabrics such as hessian which will allow you to work bigger stitches, or tight-weave fabrics such as linen which will result in smaller stitches for the same number of threads counted. If you are counting threads, always choose a fabric where the warp and weft threads are evenly woven and clearly visible.

TIP Using a blunt needle makes it easier to slip between the threads of your fabric and not split them.

Lavender Sachet

These make good stocking fillers or birthday presents for friends and family and they are amazingly quick to make. Alternatively, keep them in your own linen or clothes drawers to keep the contents smelling good. You could also attach a loop of ribbon to the sachets so you can hang them in the wardrobe.

INSTRUCTIONS

1. Cut out the two pieces of linen with pinking shears.

2. Trace the heart outline on page 91 onto card and cut it out. Find the centre of the plain piece of linen and position the heart-shaped template over it. Using the water-soluble fabric marker pen draw around the template.

3. Using the dark pink embroidery thread fill the heart with cross stitches, starting at the bottom of the heart and working upwards row by row (see pages 10–11).

4. Using the pale pink embroidery thread, stitch a line of cross stitch around the edge of the rectangle to make a frame, working about 2cm (¾in) inside the edge.

5. With wrong sides facing, pin the edges of the front and back pieces together. Using the dark pink embroidery thread, stitch a line of running stitch approximately 1.5cm (⅗in) in from the edge around all four sides of the sachet, leaving a 2cm (¾in) gap in the top edge for pouring in the lavender. Remove the pins.

6. Following the manufacturer's instructions, remove the lines of the marker pen.

7. Insert the end of the plastic funnel into the gap and pour lavender into the sachet until it is full.

8. Complete the row of running stitch to close the gap in the top of the sachet.

MATERIALS

2 pieces of linen (plain for the front and patterned for the back) measuring 12 x 14cm (4¾ x 5½in)

Pinking shears

Template

Tracing paper

Card

Pencil

Water-soluble fabric marker pen

Pale pink and dark pink embroidery thread

Needle

Scissors

Pins

Plastic funnel

Lavender

Two-Tone Stitch Tablecloth

This is a very simple cross-stitch design, but you could make it more decorative and elaborate by adding more rows of cross stitch or by cross stitching a geometric motif in the centre of the cloth. Matching napkins would complete the set – perfect for afternoon tea with the girls! (See photograph overleaf.)

INSTRUCTIONS

1. Draw a line 10cm (4in) from the edge of the cloth on all four sides using a steel ruler or measuring tape and a water-soluble fabric marker pen. This square marks the position of the base of the aqua row of cross stitches. Measure a second line 0.5cm (⅕in) above this to act as a height guide for the aqua row of cross stitches.

2. Draw another square 2cm (¾in) in from the last line to mark the base of the row of pale blue cross stitch. Measure another line 0.5cm (⅕in) above this one to act as a height guide for the pale blue cross stitches.

3. In the four corners of the square where the lines intersect, stitch a large cross using the pale blue thread in double-thread thickness (see cross stitch on pages 10–11).

4. Using a needle and the pale blue embroidery thread, and working from right to left if you are right handed and left to right if you are left handed, fill in the inner square with cross stitches, keeping the size of the stitches even and using the marked lines as a guide. Continue until all four sides are stitched.

5. Using the aqua thread, cross stitch the bottom row in the same way.

6. Following the manufacturer's instructions, remove the fabric marker pen guidelines.

MATERIALS

Tablecloth

Steel ruler

Water-soluble fabric marker pen

Pale blue and aqua embroidery thread

Needle

Scissors

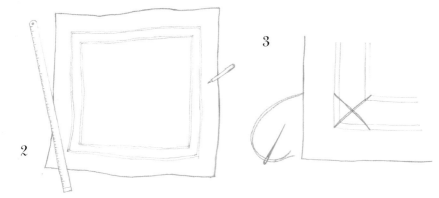

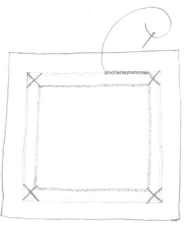

Butterfly Curtain

This pretty curtain would work well hung around a four-poster bed or at a window to diffuse light and provide privacy. Patterned multicoloured fabric has been used for the wings, but you could just as effectively use a plain fabric in a single colour. Choose a lightweight fabric that won't distort the shape of the curtain.

INSTRUCTIONS

1. Make a card template for the wings by tracing the butterfly outline on page 90 and cutting out the individual segments. Arrange these on the fabric and pin them in place, then draw around the outline using water-soluble fabric marker pen.

2. Following the manufacturer's instructions, iron the fabric onto the iron-on adhesive. Cut out the wings and put to one side. Repeat steps 1–2 to make as many pairs of wings as you need to decorate your curtain.

3. Work out the position of the butterflies on the curtain and mark each with a couple of pins. Using an embroidery hoop to keep the fabric taut and working on a flat surface, lay the curtain over the body template on page 90 so that it corresponds with the pin marks. Holding the fabric flat, use the marker pen to trace the cross-stitch pattern.

4. Using three strands of embroidery thread, fill in the butterfly body with cross stitch (see page 10). Use backstitch (see page 36) with one cross stitch at the top for the antennae.

5. Attach the wings, placing them around the cross-stitched body of the butterfly and following the manufacturer's instructions for the iron-on adhesive.

6. Repeat for the rest of the curtain, using different-coloured embroidery threads to match each pair of wings.

7. Following the manufacturer's instructions, remove the marker pen guidelines.

MATERIALS

Tracing paper and thin card to make the wings template

Assortment of light cotton fabrics for the wings

Cotton voile curtain panel

Scissors

Pins

Iron

Iron-on fabric adhesive

Water-soluble fabric marker pen

Embroidery hoop

Embroidery thread in colours co-ordinating with the fabric used for the wings

Needle

1

2

3

4

5

Blanket Stitch

Blanket Stitch

This practical stitch is most commonly used for edging hems and buttonholes. Blanket stitch is often referred to as 'buttonhole stitch' and the only difference between the two stitches is the way they are spaced. Blanket stitch has even gaps between each stitch, usually the same length as the vertical stitch. With buttonhole stitch, the stitches are worked closely together with no noticeable gap in between. For decorative work, buttonhole stitch is used to finish off scalloped edgings and to hold the threads in place for couching and overlaid work. It is also used to bind the edges in cutwork (see Drawn-Threadwork Runner on page 86).

There are many variations of blanket stitch: the gaps between stitches can be varied and the length of the straight part of the stitch may be even, uneven or arranged in groups. You can work rows of the stitch so they lie back to back or facing each other, creating an interlaced appearance. The stitch can even be worked in circles and is often used in this way for smocking or making florets.

How To Do It

Work from left to right if you are right handed and right to left if you are left handed. Bring your needle up through the fabric at A, back down at B and up again at C. Loop the thread under the needle, as shown (below left), and then pull through. Repeat for the next stitch. To finish off a line of blanket stitch make a small extra stitch on the base line to hold the last loop of blanket stitch in place.

You can also do blanket stitch along the very edge of a piece of fabric where the needle only passes through the fabric at the top points of the 'arms' – the bottom edge of the stitch binds the fabric without the needle going through it (see below right).

TIP When you are first attempting blanket stitch use a water-soluble fabric marker pen to draw a pair of parallel lines to act as a guide; these will ensure your line of stitching is both straight and even.

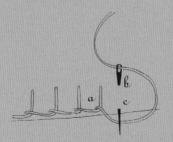

LONG-AND-SHORT BLANKET STITCH The same as blanket stitch, but the length of the arms varies (see step 4 of the Triple-Stitch Pillowcase on page 26).

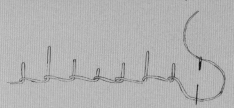

CLOSED BLANKET STITCH Bring the needle up through the start of the line at A, back down at B, as shown, up through at C and, making sure the thread is beneath the needle, pull the needle through. Take the needle back down through B and up at D, making sure the thread is beneath the needle and pull it through. This will create a triangular (closed) stitch.

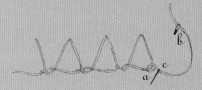

Five Project Ideas

1. Make an appliqué cushion or throw by cutting out squares of coloured fabric and joining the pieces together using buttonhole stitch. Decorate each square with smaller squares or circles placed one on top of the other and secure in place by stitching around the edges with blanket stitch.

2. Decorate a muslin or voile curtain with florets of blanket stitch (blanket stitch sewn in a circle instead of a straight line). Use white embroidery thread on white fabric for a delicate, pretty look.

3. Decorate pillowcases by stitching two rows of interlaced buttonhole stitch around the edges. For a denser border, sew a single row of buttonhole stitch.

4. Cut out an oval shape from felt, cut it in half and then stitch the two pieces together with contrasting coloured blanket stitch to make cheerful egg cosies.

5. Using the same method as above, cut out pieces of felt to make finger puppets, joining the pieces together with blanket stitch. Children can then decorate them using wool and fabric glue to make the hair and a fabric pen to draw faces.

Blanket-Stitch Throw

This project is really simple and fast – so a good one to do when relaxing in front of the television. A colourful line of blanket stitch such as this can lift a dull throw and will help to co-ordinate it with a colour scheme. Don't restrict the use of blanket stitch to blankets – sheets, quilts, napkins and tablecloths can all be edged with this stitch.

MATERIALS

Bright blue blanket or throw

Lime green embroidery thread

Needle

Scissors

INSTRUCTIONS

1. Work from left to right if you are right handed and right to left if you are left handed, with the tip of the needle and the edge of the throw towards you. Knot the end of the thread and bring out the needle near the lower edge of the throw in one corner.

2. Insert the needle through the fabric from the right side, approximately 1cm (½in) to the right and equidistant from the edge of the throw. Bring the needle out at the edge directly below this point, keeping the thread from the previous stitch under the tip of the needle, and draw the needle and thread through. Repeat this stitch, keeping the stitches the same size and equally distanced.

3. When you reach the end of this row, finish off by knotting the thread on the reverse, then stitch along the other edge in the same way.

TIP If you prefer, work the blanket stitch along the very edge of the blanket or throw, where the needle only passes through the fabric at the top points of the arms and the bottom edge of the stitch binds the fabric (see page 22).

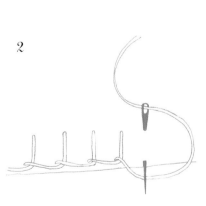

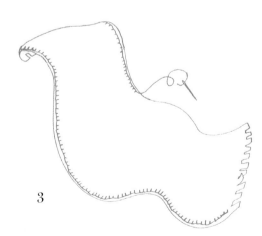

Triple-Stitch Pillowcase

This pillowcase has been decorated with a line of ordinary blanket stitch, a line of long-and-short blanket stitch and a line of closed blanket stitch. Each of these rows also has a whipped lower edge to make it thicker and a little more decorative.

MATERIALS

Pillowcase

Water-soluble fabric marker pen

Steel ruler

Embroidery thread

Needle

Blunt needle

Scissors

INSTRUCTIONS

1. Using the fabric marker pen and steel ruler, draw three lines the width of the pillowcase just in from one of its edges and spaced 2cm (¾in) apart.

2. Following the first line, stitch a row of basic blanket stitch (see page 22).

3. To whip the lower edge of this row of stitching, use the blunt needle and embroidery thread and, working from left to right if you are right handed and right to left if you are left handed, pass the needle under the lower thread of each blanket stitch from top to bottom, as shown, without piercing the fabric.

4. Stitch a row of long-and-short blanket stitch above the first row. If you are nervous about doing this freehand, draw it out with the fabric marker pen. This stitch works in exactly the same way as blanket stitch, but you vary the length of the arms (see page 22). Here, we have used a repeating group of five stitches that graduate in size, measuring 0.5cm (⅛in), 1cm (⅖in), 1.5cm (⅗in), 1cm (⅖in), and 0.5cm (⅛in). Each stitch is spaced 0.5cm (⅛in) apart.

5. Whip the bottom edge of the long-and-short blanket stitching, as before.

6. Stitch a row of closed blanket stitch along the third and last row (see page 23). Instead of creating vertical parallel arms, you create alternately slanting arms with the needle entering the fabric at the same central point on subsequent stitches to form a triangle shape.

7. Following the manufacturer's instructions, remove the fabric marker guidelines.

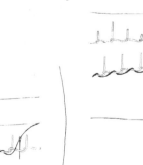

Blanket-Stitch Tote Bag

If making a bag from scratch sounds too time-consuming, you can always decorate a bought bag with a blanket-stitched edge. Or, make a bag out of a strong, non-fraying fabric such as felt or vinyl and miss out the self-lining steps, instead just machine-stitching the pieces together and decorating the edges with blanket stitch.

MATERIALS

Fabric

Scissors

Ruler or tape measure

Pins

Sewing machine

Matching sewing thread

Iron

Embroidery thread

Needle

INSTRUCTIONS

1. Fold the fabric in half with right sides together and cut out all the pieces. You need: four pieces of 30 x 25cm (12 x 10in) for the front and back; two pieces of 82 x 18cm (32½ x 7in) for the gusset; and four pieces of 60 x 2.5cm (24 x 1in) for the handles.

2. With right sides facing, pin the two front panels of the bag together, allowing a 0.5cm (⅛in) seam. Stitch on the machine leaving a 4cm (1½in) gap on one edge so it can be turned right sides out. Repeat for the back panels of the bag.

3. For the gusset, fold the fabric with right sides facing and, allowing a 0.5cm (⅛in) hem as before, stitch around the edges, leaving one end open so the fabric can be turned right sides out. Do the same for both handles. Press open the seams, then turn the pieces right sides out, slipstitch the open edges closed and press once again.

4. Pin the front of the bag to the gusset piece so the seams are on the outside of the bag with a 0.5cm (⅛in) seam allowance; then topstitch on the machine. Attach the back panel of the bag to the other side of the gusset in the same way.

5. Measure 5cm (2in) in from each top edge and position the handles on the inside of the bag to a depth of 3cm (1¼in). Pin in place and machine-stitch.

6. Using three strands of embroidery thread, blanket stitch around the opening of the bag, working the blanket stitch over the edge of the seam so that the bottom part of the stitch binds the edge of the fabric (see page 22). Repeat for the exposed seams on the front and back of the bag.

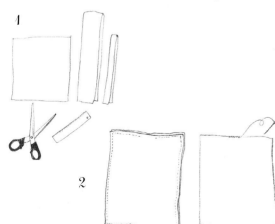

Line & Chain Stitch

Line & Chain Stitch

Line stitch, or running stitch, is the most commonly used and the simplest stitch of all. There are many variations on this stitch: a row of tiny, barely visible stitches is known as 'prick stitch'; long, even running stitches are used for tacking (or basting) pieces of fabric together; and near-solid stitches, with barely any gap in between (such as those done on a sewing), create a strong, stable stitch. For decorative embroidery, running stitch is used as a single row or in a series of lines to fill in large areas.

Chain stitch is a loop of thread held in place with a small stitch. It is a handy and versatile stitch and, like running stitch, can be worked both as a line or to fill large areas. It is widely used in traditional Chinese and Indian embroidery where it is often worked using a hook instead of a needle.

How To Do It

RUNNING STITCH If you are right handed work the stitches from right to left, and if you are left handed from left to right. Bring the needle up through the fabric at A and down at B to make one complete stitch. To make the next stitch, bring the needle back up through the fabric at C and repeat as before.

Several stitches can be lined up on the needle at one time before pulling it through the fabric. This is the fastest and most efficient way to sew running stitch.

TIP For a neat row of running stitch, make sure each stitch is the same length and that the gaps between stitches are even.

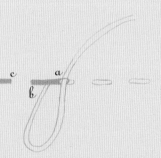

BACKSTITCH This is worked in a straight line. Bring your needle up through the fabric, take a small stitch backwards and then bring the needle back up through the fabric an equal distance in front of where you started. Repeat to fill the row.

CHAIN STITCH Working from right to left or from top to bottom, bring the needle up through the fabric at A and then insert it again in the same place. Without pulling the thread through, bring the needle back through the fabric a short distance away at B and loop the thread under the needle as shown, then pull it through. To make the next link in the chain, re-insert the needle at B and bring the needle back through the fabric at C, looping the thread around the needle as shown. Repeat until the row of chain stitch is complete.

TIP Keep chain stitches relatively short in length so they have a pleasing, rounded shape – if the stitch is too long it will start to look spidery.

Five Project Ideas

1. Create a polka-dot effect on an A-line skirt by working solid circles of chain stitch in a range of colours. For fine materials use silk embroidery thread and for thicker wool-based fabric use canvas wool. You could decorate a matching silk evening bag in the same way. To keep the design interesting, vary the size of the circles.

2. Work individual chain stitches in a circle from a central point to create a small flower motif. Use these stitches to decorate a flowing kaftan-style top, clustering them around the neckline, cuffs and lower hem.

3. Work five rows of chain stitch in different colours around the flat edge of an Oxford pillowcase and along the top edge of a sheet to create stylish bed linen.

4. Trace the outline of a floral pattern onto a piece of fabric and, using one or two strands of embroidery thread, pick out the design with chain stitch. Make the piece of fabric up into a cushion cover or stitch it onto one side of a bag.

5. Chain stitch is easily worked to form a scroll shape, so using shades of blue and turquoise decorate the edge of a blind in a bathroom with wave-like scrolls.

Running-Stitch Cushion

This project uses running stitch that is built up row after row to create a simple pattern. Here, ordinary embroidery thread has been used, but tapestry wool could be used as an alternative to create a chunkier effect. Think creatively about your choice of colours – this cushion features two shades of brown thread – chocolate and rust – that tone with the colour of the cushion cover and an orange-yellow that stands out and helps lift the other colours.

MATERIALS

Plain cushion cover

Ruler or tape measure

Pins

Coloured embroidery threads

Embroidery needle

Scissors

INSTRUCTIONS

1. Measure 0.5cm (⅛in) down from the top edge of the cushion cover and pin a straight line across the top of the cushion to act as a guide for sewing.

2. Starting from the top of the cushion, and working from right to left if you are right handed and left to right if you are left handed, sew a line of running stitch across the top of the cushion (following the instructions on page 36). Try to keep your stitches even and follow the line of pins to keep your stitches straight.

3. Stitch the next row in the same way, 1cm (⅜in) down from the first row.

4. Build up several rows of one colour and then switch to another so that the overall effect isn't too regimented.

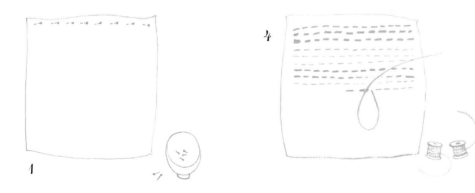

Chain-Stitch Napkin

Plain napkins are relatively inexpensive to buy and you can personalize them by adding a few simple rows of stitching. Alternatively, make your own by hemming squares of thick cotton or linen fabric. This project uses metallic thread, which can be a little tricky to work with at first, so practise on a scrap of cloth before starting on your new crisp napkins.

MATERIALS

Napkin

Metallic thread

Needle

Scissors

Coin

Water-soluble fabric marker pen

INSTRUCTIONS

1. Thread three strands of metallic thread onto a needle and knot the end. Starting in one corner of the napkin, bring the needle through to the right side about 1.5cm (⅜in) from the edge. Then, without pulling the thread through, insert it again in the same place and bring it back through the fabric a short distance to the left (if you are right handed and working from right to left). Loop the thread under the tip of the needle as shown and then draw it through (see also page 37).

2. To make the next link in the chain, re-insert the needle just behind the point where the thread emerges and bring it back through the fabric a stitch-length away, looping the thread under the needle as before. Repeat until you have chain stitched all around the edge of the napkin.

3. Position a coin in one corner of the napkin and draw around it using a water-soluble fabric pen.

4. Following the technique described above, chain stitch around the circle.

5. Following the manufacturer's instructions for the fabric marker pen, remove the drawn outline.

TIP You may find it easier to work chain stitch from top to bottom.

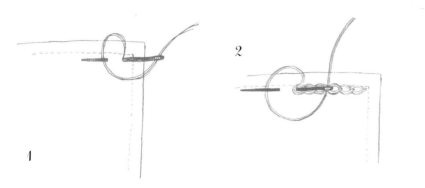

Daisy-Chain Scarf

Chain stitch has been used in this project to create a scattered daisy design to decorate the ends of a scarf. You can either use an existing scarf and line it with matching fabric to conceal the back of the stitching, or you can make one from scratch, using silk or a light wool fabric.

INSTRUCTIONS

1. Trace the daisy design on page 91 onto your fabric or scarf, clustering the flower heads together at the bottom end. If your fabric is translucent, then you should be able to trace over the template with the fabric marker pen. If you are using a dark or thick fabric then you will need to trace the design onto dressmaker's carbon paper (following the manufacturer's instructions) and then transfer it onto the fabric.

2. Stretch the fabric into an embroidery hoop, which will make sewing easier. Using three strands of embroidery thread, outline the petals and flower centres with chain stitch (see page 37). Start each flower at the tip of one petal and work your way all around the edge, finishing in the centre of each flower. Sew some flowers in green thread, some in grey and some in cream.

3. When the entire motif has been stitched, remove the marker pen or carbon outline following the manufacturer's instructions.

4. Using the sewing machine, zigzag stitch the raw edges of the lining fabric. Turn under the hem allowance at both short ends, then pin, tack and machine-stitch; remove the tacking and press. With right sides together, place the lining fabric on the scarf and pin, tack and then machine-stitch the side seams. Remove the tacking, press the seams open and turn the scarf right sides out. Leave the ends open or slipstitch the lining to the scarf.

MATERIAL

Scarf or wrap

Template

Water-soluble fabric marker pen or dressmaker's carbon paper

Embroidery hoop

Embroidery thread in green, cream and grey

Needle

Scissors

Lining fabric, cut to the same dimensions as your scarf with a 1cm (⅜in) seam allowance all round

Pins

Tacking thread

Sewing machine

Matching sewing thread

Iron

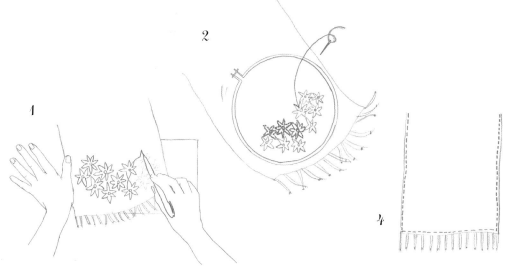

Satin Stitch

Satin Stitch

Predominantly used to fill small and medium-sized areas, satin stitch creates a super-smooth and solid surface. The stitch can be worked in different ways so that it catches the light and creates subtle, shaded effects. Perfected by the Chinese who use it for many of their pictorial embroideries, it is used to illustrate flowers such as carnations and the more delicate branches of cherry blossom. Soaring birds, chasing dragons and leaping fish are all picked out in this sumptuous stitch.

To create more of a raised effect, satin stitch is usually worked over an outline of running stitch, which is then in-filled with herringbone stitch. The projects shown in this chapter use a less traditional and faster method, replacing the herringbone stitch with iron-on interfacing, creating more or less the same results.

How To Do It

Work from left to right if you are right handed and right to left if you are left handed. Start by bringing the needle up through the thread at A and down at B. Then bring the needle back up through the fabric at C and back down at D. Then bring the needle back up at E and continue to fill the area required. Stitches should lie as close together as possible with no fabric showing in between. On evenly woven fabric you can work stitches horizontally, vertically or in a slanted direction, in which case choose the direction of the slant to suit the shape of the motif you are working. If the stitches become too long they will not lie flat.

TIPS Having worked the stitches, stroke them with the tip of a needle to settle them into place. For a smooth, glossy finish use stranded cotton thread. For an ultra-crisp edge mark your outlines with a smooth line of stitching, and always insert the needle on the same side of your marker outline.

Five Project Ideas

1. Take design inspiration from the simple flower designs of Eastern European embroidery and transfer your favourite motif onto a purse and fill in the petals with brightly coloured satin stitch.

2. You can use satin stitch to create monogrammed bed linen; if doing this, one idea is to give the stitching the style of a coat of arms. Start by incorporating a decorative motif in the design, such as a bird or entwined branches. Then find a script that you like, enlarge it on a photocopier and trace it onto the fabric. Keep the look traditional by embroidering white on white.

3. Satin stitch can be worked in geometric squares to create a checkerboard effect – use this to decorate the four corners of a tablecloth or napkins.

4. There is no need to always use traditional patterns, so why not copy a retro design from the 1960s – big and bold *Magic Roundabout*-style flowers would look great picked out in satin stitch on a brightly coloured skirt or jacket.

5. Decorate the sash of a silk dressing gown with satin-stitch leaves and trailing foliage; if you are feeling adventurous you could also work on the pockets or cuffs of the gown.

Polka-Dot Cushion

If you have never before attempted satin stitch, this is a good project to start with. Polka-dots are one of the simplest and most effective patterns, always looking fresh and modern. Here, a textured cushion cover has been used with some of the colours in the weave picked out to create the dots.

MATERIALS

Pencil

Cotton reel

Iron-on interfacing

Scissors

Tape measure or ruler

Pins

Cushion cover

Iron

Three shades of embroidery thread

Needle

INSTRUCTIONS

1. Using a pencil and the end of a cotton reel, draw nine circles on the iron-on interfacing and cut them out. These will act as a guide for sewing and will slightly raise the polka-dots from the surface of the cushion.

2. Using a tape measure or ruler, work out the position of each polka-dot and pin the interfacing circles in place, making sure they are spaced at regular intervals. Attach them to the cushion using the iron and following the manufacturer's instructions.

3. Plan which colour embroidery thread will be used for each polka-dot. Then, using two strands of your chosen thread, backstitch all the way around the edge of each of the interfacing circles (see page 36).

4. Starting in the centre of each circle, work outwards to fill the first half with satin stitch (see page 50), decreasing the length of each stitch gradually to stay within the edge of the circle. Make sure you pull the thread evenly so that it lies flat and there are no gaps between the stitches. Repeat to fill the other half of the circle.

5. Stitch the rest of the circles in the same way, making sure the satin stitches all run in the same direction.

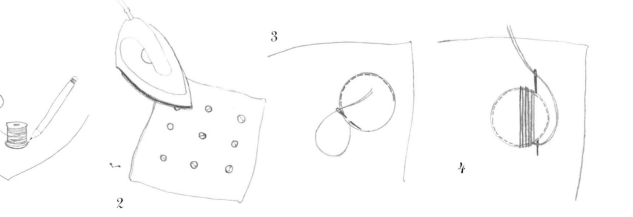

Hipster Belt

Dress up a pair of jeans or give a dress an ultra-feminine look with this embroidered belt worked in a 1930s colour palette. The classic rose stem is a versatile design and you can apply it to a variety of items. Use it to decorate a bag or scarf, or – if you have the time – work it around the hem of a skirt.

INSTRUCTIONS

1. If you are using a ready-made belt, unpick one side seam near the end so you can slide your hand in and ensure you stitch through one layer of fabric only. To make the belt, cut a strip of fabric long enough to tie around your hips and the desired width, plus a 1.5cm (⅝in) hem allowance all round. Cut the lining fabric to the same size.

2. Trace the rose template on page 90 onto the iron-on interfacing and cut it out. Pin it in position on the right side of the belt and, following the manufacturer's instructions, iron the interfacing in place to attach it.

3. Using the palest shade of green thread, fill in the stems with satin stitch, making sure that your stitches lie horizontally across the fabric (see page 50).

4. Fill in the leaves with satin stitch using the darker green thread. Start at the tip or base of the leaf and work outwards – this will help to ensure a smooth edge.

5. Use different shades of yellow and orange thread to fill in each segment of the flower with satin stitch, starting by filling in the top segment using the palest shade.

6. If you have used a ready-made belt, slipstitch the opening closed. To make the belt, pin the fabric and lining together with right sides facing, tack and then stitch three edges, leaving one short edge unstitched. Remove the tacking, press the seams open and turn right sides out. Turn under the hem allowance on the open edge and slipstitch closed.

MATERIALS

Fabric belt, or fabric and lining to make a belt

Scissors

Template

Water-soluble fabric marker pen

Iron-on interfacing

Pins

Iron

Needle

Two shades of green embroidery thread

Two shades of orange and yellow embroidery thread

Matching sewing thread

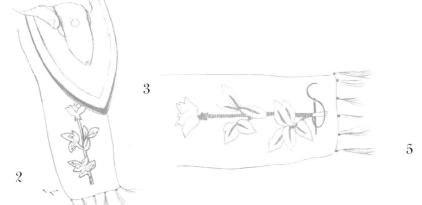

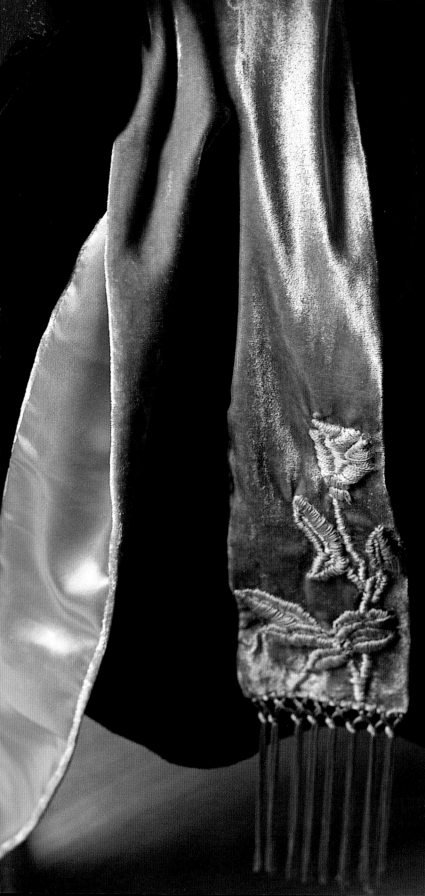

Floral Skirt

This floral design is based on a 1920s textile. If you are feeling ambitious you could repeat the design all around the lower edge or work it diagonally across the skirt, starting just below the hip and finishing at the hem on the opposite side. The possibilities are endless, only limited by how much time you have.

INSTRUCTIONS

1. Trace the design on page 91 onto the iron-on interfacing with the fabric marker pen.

2. Carefully cut out the stems, leaves and berries. Then cut out the flowers. Cut around the outer edge of the design, keeping the flower design intact. Don't cut out the individual segments as it will be impossible to position them correctly on the skirt.

3. Pin the two flower heads in place first, then arrange the stems, leaves and berries using the original design as a guide. Following the manufacturer's instructions, iron the interfacing in place.

4. Using an embroidery hoop to make sure the fabric is taut, start by filling in the stems and leaves with satin stitch worked in pale blue thread (see page 50).

5. Fill in the berries, using pale blue thread for the fruit and pale grey for the leaves.

6. Use pale grey thread to fill in the flower petals. Make sure you work the satin stitch so that the direction of the stitches gradually fans outwards from the centre of each segment – avoid changing direction abruptly.

7. When you have completed both flowers, use fine, sharp embroidery scissors to cut away the interfacing between each petal, taking care not to cut the skirt fabric or stitching (keep the design in the embroidery hoop as you do this).

8. Remove the embroidery hoop and press the design on the reverse, placing a towel under the embroidered section – this will prevent the embroidery from being flattened and will remove any marks left by the embroidery hoop.

MATERIALS

Template

Iron-on interfacing

Water-soluble fabric marker pen

Fine embroidery scissors

Pins

Skirt

Iron

Embroidery hoop

Pale blue and pale grey embroidery thread

Needle

TIP Experiment with colour combinations – this pattern would also look good worked in deep shades of crimson and pink, golden yellow with orange, or soft purple and aubergine.

3

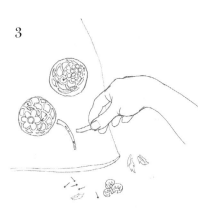

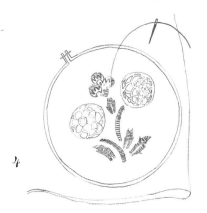

7

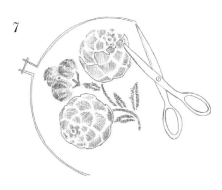

Feather Stitch

Feather Stitch

This light and delicate stitch is often used on smocking for decoration and to create the smocking itself. Its linear nature means that it can also be used for backgrounds and to make borders. There are many types of feather stitch: single feather stitch is similar to blanket stitch except the arms are angled instead of straight; while double feather stitch is worked in a zigzag pattern, which gives it an almost lacy effect (see the Double Feather-Stitch Pyjamas on page 68). Fly stitch is another form of feather stitch, which can be used to create elegant leaf- and feather-shaped motifs (see the Feather-Stitch Sequin Scarf on page 72).

How To Do It

Working from top to bottom, bring the needle up through the fabric at A and back down at B, then out again at C without pulling it all the way through. Leaving the needle still inserted in the fabric, loop the thread under the needle tip as shown and pull the needle through to create your first stitch.

To make the next stitch, take the needle down through the fabric at D (to the left) and back up again at E, looping the thread under the needle, as shown, and pull through. Continue making stitches alternately to the right and left until the row is finished. To finish off a row hold the last loop in place with a small stitch.

TIP To create an even line of stitches ensure the distance between A and B and B and C is consistent.

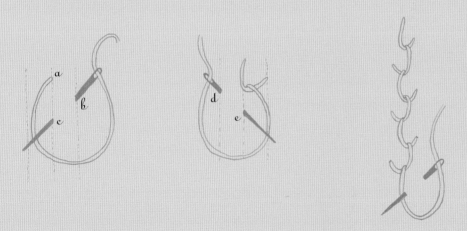

Five Project Ideas

1. Use fly stitch to decorate a gauzy curtain panel with falling leaves. Start at the top of the curtain, decorating it with well-spaced-out small leaves that have a curved shape and are positioned at different angles to give the impression that they are in motion. As you work down the curtain make the leaves bigger and position them closer together so that you have a dense mass of piled leaves at the very bottom. Use three to five shades of embroidery thread in similar tones.

2. Play with contrasting materials; a towelling robe can be made more decorative and stylish by embroidering the opening edges and cuffs with a row of double feather stitch in silky embroidery thread.

3. Feather stitch is fast to work, so use it to personalize gifts for friends as well as pieces for yourself. Work three to five rows (odd numbers always look better) around the edge of a tablecloth or a set of napkins. For a traditional country feel, work in shades of red or pink on white linen. For something a bit more modern, stitch black and silver onto a grey cloth or cream and dark chocolate onto beige napkins.

4. You can make feather stitch using wool, too. Just decorate the band of a woolly hat with double feather stitch and glue on some sequins for a bit of cosy glamour. Use a blunt needle with a large eye so that it is easy to thread. You could also decorate the cuffs of a pair of woollen gloves in this way.

5. Feather stitch can be used to decorate the seams of patchwork cushions. Use a unifying colour and work around the edges of each patch to give it even more homemade rustic charm.

Feather-Stitch Bag

This is one of those rewarding projects where a minimum of time and effort will produce great results – once you get a good rhythm going, feather stitch is amazingly fast to do. A combination of feather stitch and running stitch is used – running stitch is worked in wool along the edges of the bag and handle while feather stitch, worked in embroidery thread, adds detail to the border and pocket.

INSTRUCTIONS

1. Using the tapestry wool, stitch a row of running stitch along both edges of the bag handles, the top edges of the bag and around the pocket flap (if your bag has one).

2. Using a ruler or tape measure and a fabric marker pen, draw a central line around the border of the bag to act as a guide for the line of feather stitch. Draw similar lines wherever else on the bag you wish to sew a line of feather stitch. Here, three fanned lines have been drawn on the pocket flap.

3. Turn the bag on its side so that you can work the row of feather stitches from top to bottom using the embroidery thread (see page 64). Keep your stitches even in size and equidistant from the central guide line.

4. Do the same on the pocket flap, working each line of feather stitch from top to bottom.

5. Following the manufacturer's instructions, remove the fabric marker pen guide lines.

(see page 64)

MATERIALS

Bag

Brown tapestry wool

Brown embroidery thread

Needle

Scissors

Ruler or tape measure

Water-soluble fabric marker pen

TIP When stitching, make sure the needle does not pass through to the back of the bag. Work your stitches so that they only catch the top layer of fabric and leave the reverse neat.

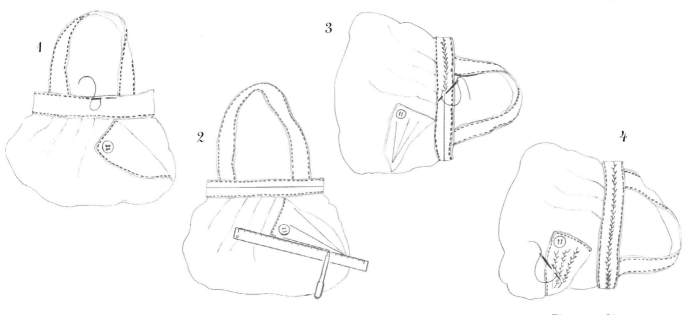

Double Feather-Stitch Pyjamas

This project builds on the technique used for the Feather-Stitch Bag on page 66. Double feather stitch has a zigzag pattern, making it good for decorating borders and edges. Here the stitch is worked freehand using the natural stripe in the fabric as a guide. If you would prefer your stitches to be perfectly even, then you will need to draw four parallel lines on the fabric.

MATERIALS

Pyjamas

Ruler or tape measure

Water-soluble fabric marker pen

Grey embroidery thread

Needle

Scissors

INSTRUCTIONS

1. Starting with the pyjama top, using a ruler or tape measure and a water-soluble fabric marker pen, draw four parallel lines 1cm (½in) apart, the first 2cm (¾in) in from the edge of the cuff.

2. Using the standard technique for feather stitch, turn the fabric so you can work the stitch from top to bottom (see page 64 for more details). Starting on the far left-hand line, bring the needle up through the fabric at A. Then insert the needle at B on the adjacent line and at the same height. Then bring it up again directly below at C. Make sure the loop of thread is beneath the tip of the needle and then draw the thread through.

3. Make two more feather stitches diagonally down and to the right of this first stitch, each time inserting the needle at the same height as the emerging thread and on the adjacent line. You should now have a line of three stitches that lie diagonally from left down to right.

4. Make three more feather stitches, this time working diagonally down and to the left in the same way as before.

5. Continue working around the cuff of the pyjamas, making two stitches to the left and then two stitches to the right until you reach the point at which you started.

6. Repeat for the remaining arm and leg cuffs and the breast pocket of the pyjamas.

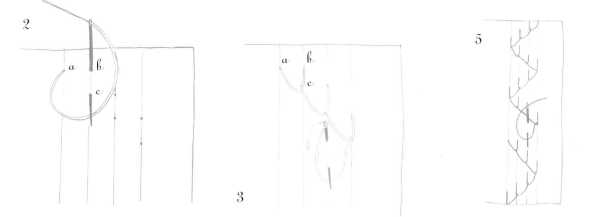

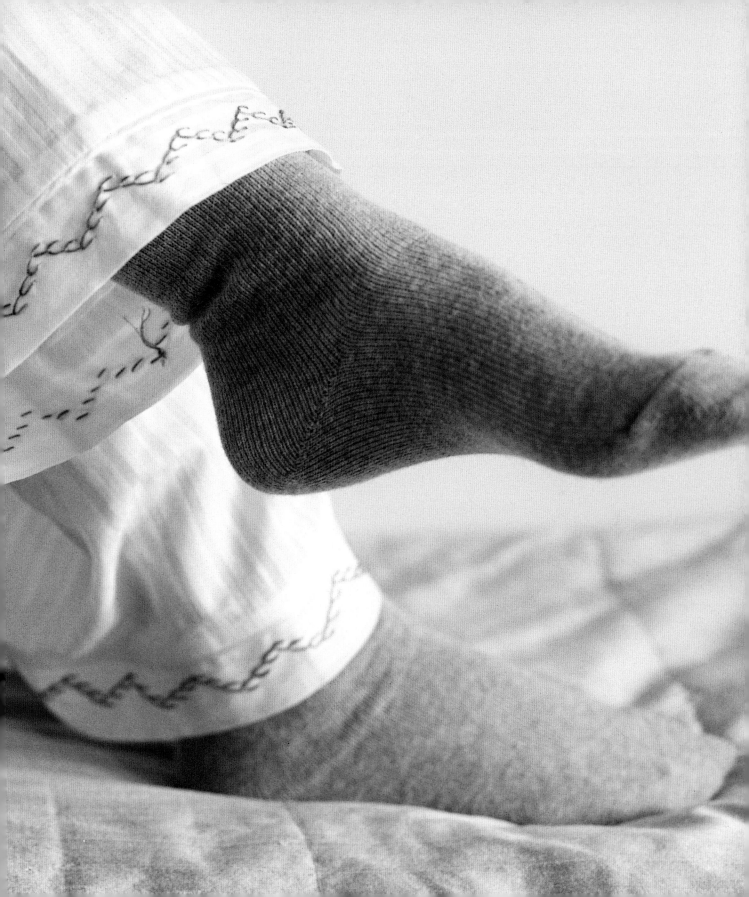

Feather-Stitch Sequin Scarf

The leaf and feather motifs used here are made by using closed fly stitch, which is a member of the feather-stitch family (see photograph overleaf). Try practising this stitch on a piece of scrap fabric before you start work as many different effects can be achieved. For example, the central line of the motif can be curved and the outer stitches can be all the same length, fanned, evenly spaced or worked next to each other to create a solid shape.

MATERIALS

Scarf

Pins

Three shades of embroidery thread

Needle

Scissors

Sequins

Fabric glue

Lining fabric (optional)

INSTRUCTIONS

1. Roughly work out where you want to position your leaves on the scarf and insert pins to mark the top and bottom points of each one, varying the sizes and shapes of the leaves to keep the design interesting.

2. Working the leaf from top to bottom, bring your needle up at A at the central top point of the leaf, and down at B, directly below this, making a small straight stitch. Then bring the needle back up again at C.

3. Take the needle down at D directly opposite C and at an equal distance from the central stitch, and up at E just beneath B. Make sure the loop of thread lies under the tip of the needle, as shown, and pull it through to make the top three stitches of your leaf.

4. Take the needle directly down from E to F to make another straight stitch. Then bring it up at G, to the left and almost at the same height as E. Keeping the thread beneath the tip of the needle, bring the needle down at H, directly opposite G and bring it up again just beneath F.

5. Continue down the length of the leaf and finish with a long central straight stitch that resembles a stalk.

6. When you have sewn all your leaves, randomly scatter sequins over the design and glue them in place.

7. If you would like to hide the stitches on the reverse of the scarf for a more perfect finish, line just the lower section with lining fabric. Measure the dimensions of the stitched area of the scarf and add a 1.5cm (⅜in) hem all round. Press the seam allowance under and either topstitch or slipstitch the lining (wrong sides together) onto the back of the scarf. Lining it in this way will prevent any chunky seams and avoid making your scarf narrower.

TIP When you are working larger leaves it is easier to use a longer needle that will stretch to the tip of the leaves.

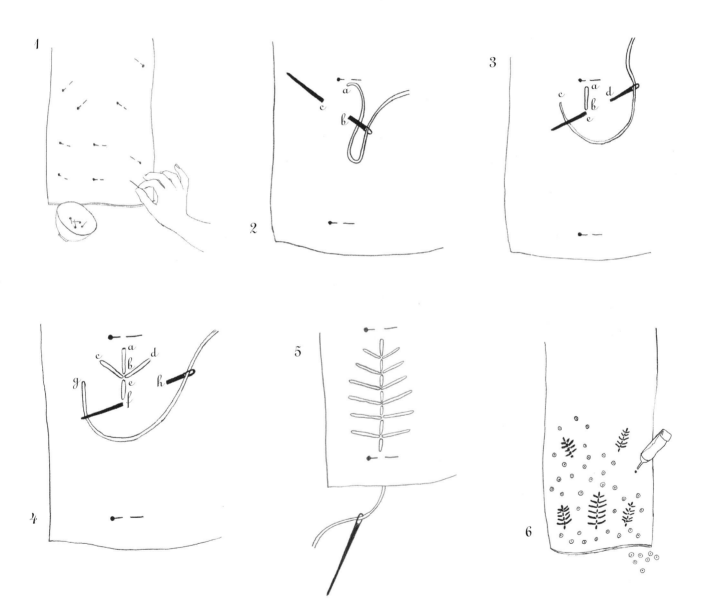

Insertion Stitch

Insertion Stitch & Drawn Threadwork

INSERTION STITCH Sometimes called 'faggoting', insertion stitch is used to join two pieces of material in a decorative way. There are a range of different stitches you can use, from the simple laced effect of herringbone stitch to the more elaborate and woven-looking finish of Italian insertion stitch. Most insertion stitches leave a slight gap between the fabrics being joined and this can be exaggerated with larger stitches to create an almost lacy effect.

Usually the edges of the fabrics you are joining together need to be turned under and hemmed or lined, unless you are joining together widths of ribbon or braid. Use a slightly thicker thread than your fabric to emphasize the stitching, and avoid using stranded thread.

How To Do It

LACED INSERTION STITCH Working from right to left, bring the needle up through the edge of the fabric and twist the thread around the needle as shown (below left). Then insert the needle back through the fabric, looping the thread under the needle. Repeat, working to the left and keeping the size of the stitches even.

To lace the loops together using contrasting thread, insert the needle up through the hem at one end of the row of loops and then take it down through the first loop on the opposite side. Then take the needle up through the first loop on the side you started on. Continue lacing contrasting thread through opposite loops until you reach the end of the row and then tie off the thread (below right).

TIP Tack the two pieces of fabric you are joining onto a sheet of brown paper about 6–12mm (¼–½in) apart – this will stop them from moving around and means that your stitches will be even.

DRAWN THREADWORK This is worked in exactly the way that its name suggests, by pulling threads from a piece of material and then securing the ones left by gathering them into clusters with embroidery stitches such as spoke stitch (see page 79) to make regular patterns. Used to decorate bedspreads, sheets, pillows, towels, tablecloths, mats, napkins and curtains, it is also used to make decorative hems and borders on clothing. Traditionally it is worked with white thread on a white fabric ground, but there is no reason why you shouldn't experiment with coloured threads – see the projects on pages 82 and 86 for inspiration.

SPOKE STITCH Work from right to left if you are right handed and left to right if you are left handed. Bring the needle from left to right in front of three vertical threads and then pass it back to the left behind the threads and pull to create a bundle (A). Take the needle back over to the right of the bundle and insert the needle up through the edge of hem as shown (B) and pull the thread taut, creating a crossed-over stitch. Repeat to the right until the row is finished.

You can also create decorative motifs using this technique in the style of Sicilian and Russian embroidery. Before you withdraw any threads, stitch the outline of your motif in buttonhole stitch. Then, to prevent the fabric from warping, remove two warp threads, leave a gap of two and then remove the next two. Repeat this process for the weft threads, removing two rows of thread and leaving two rows of thread.

TIP Good fabrics to use include linen and loosely woven woollens.

Five Project Ideas

1. Decorate a top or skirt with rows of deep lace that are joined together with insertion stitches.

2. Transform a loosely woven mohair scarf by pulling out threads along its length to create an open, lacy border. Secure the threads with knotted border stitch (see page 82) and stitch a row of beads or sequins along either side of the border.

3. To make a decorative curtain panel use insertion stitch to join widths of linen – choose brightly coloured fabric such as lime green with contrasting stitching in hot pink or orange. For a subtler effect, work white thread on white fabric.

4. Insertion stitch can be used to join together the two halves of a tea cosy. Use a contrasting colour and thicker thread than the fabric to ensure it stands out as a decorative feature.

5. Decorate a linen tablecloth with drawn threadwork motifs such as butterflies, simple animal shapes or geometric patterns, using the method described on page 78. Space them evenly over the cloth so that when it is spread over a table one area isn't more heavily decorated than another.

Laced Placemat

Insertion stitch is a decorative stitch that is used traditionally as a means of joining two pieces of fabric together. There are many variations, but the laced insertion stitch used here is one of the simplest. You could also use it to add borders to tablecloths and napkins.

MATERIALS

Blue fabric

Scissors

Sewing machine

Matching sewing thread

Iron

Pins

Turquoise and pink
embroidery thread

Needle

INSTRUCTIONS

1. To make the placemat, cut out the back piece measuring 42 x 34cm (16½ x 13½in), the front middle section measuring 34 x 23cm (13½ x 9in) and two side sections measuring 34 x 11cm (13½ x 4½in). Sew the raw edges using zigzag machine stitch.

2. Press under a 1cm (⅜in) hem allowance on the middle front section along both of the longest edges and topstitch. Repeat for one long edge on each of the side panels.

3. Allowing a 1cm (½in) seam and with right sides together, pin the two side panels to the back piece of the placemat, lining them up with the edges. Make sure the topstitched edges of the side panels are lying towards the centre of the placemat. Sew the top, bottom and outer side seams, using running stitch on the machine.

4. With right sides facing, pin the middle panel centrally between the side panels and machine-stitch along the top and bottom edges, allowing a 1cm (½in) hem.

5. Press all seams open and then turn the placemat right sides out.

6. Thread the needle with turquoise embroidery thread and sew a row of knotted loops along the four loose edges of the slits in the placemat. Bring the needle up through the edge of the fabric and twist the thread around the needle. Insert the needle back through the fabric, looping the thread under the tip, then pull it tight (see page 78). Keep the stitches and loops the same size and make sure that the loops in facing rows fall directly opposite each other so they can be laced together.

7. To lace the loops using the pink embroidery thread, insert the needle up through the hem at one end of the loops and take it down through the first loop on the opposite side. Then take the needle up through the first loop on the side on which you started. Continue lacing the contrasting thread through opposite loops until you reach the end of the row and then tie off the thread. Repeat for the other side of the placemat.

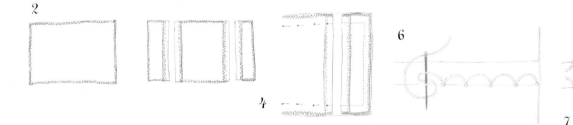

Drawn-Threadwork Throw

Traditionally drawn threadwork is executed on fine linen – such needlework requires excellent eyesight and the patience of a saint. To speed things up and provide more instant results, use a loosely woven woollen throw instead. As the name suggests, this project involves removing weft threads and embroidering the remaining warp threads to create a pretty lacy pattern (see photographs overleaf).

MATERIALS

Loosely woven pale pink throw

Steel ruler or measuring tape

Pins

Sharp embroidery scissors

Brown embroidery thread

Blunt needle

INSTRUCTIONS

1. Start by removing the weft threads (the horizontal threads as the fabric was woven) from sections of the throw. Measure 6cm (2⅓in) from the bottom edge of the throw and mark with pins. Using the scissors, carefully cut the weft thread marked by the pin and start to un-weave it. Make several more cuts along the length of the same thread so that you can pull it out in sections. Remove four more threads above the first in the same way.

2. Count another five weft threads up from the last thread removed and mark with pins. Using the same method remove another five threads, working upwards as before.

3. For the last section, count five weft threads up from the last thread removed and, using the same method, remove the next ten weft threads.

4. Knotted border stitch is used to embroider the remaining warp threads (the vertical threads as the fabric was woven). Thread a blunt needle with brown embroidery thread and secure the thread in the centre at the start of the first row of warp thread. Working from right to left, pass the needle under four of the warp threads, loop the thread over the tip of the needle, as shown, and pull tight. Repeat to the end of the row and secure the thread.

5. Repeat for the second section of warp-only threads.

6. On the final extra-wide row of warp thread you need to work two rows of knotted border stitch. To make your first row secure the thread one third of the way up the right-hand edge and work a row of knotted border stitch in the same way as in previous rows.

7. To work a second row of knotted border stitch, start two thirds of the way up the side edge. Pass the needle under two warp threads, looping the thread over the tip of the needle and pulling tight as before. Then pass the needle under the next four warp threads, looping the thread over the tip of the needle and pulling tight. Continue passing the needle under bundles of four threads until you reach the end of the row and secure the thread.

8. To add extra detail, work four rows of running stitch in brown embroidery thread on the two sections of fabric between the drawn-thread sections.

9. Repeat the above steps to create the same pattern at the other end of the throw.

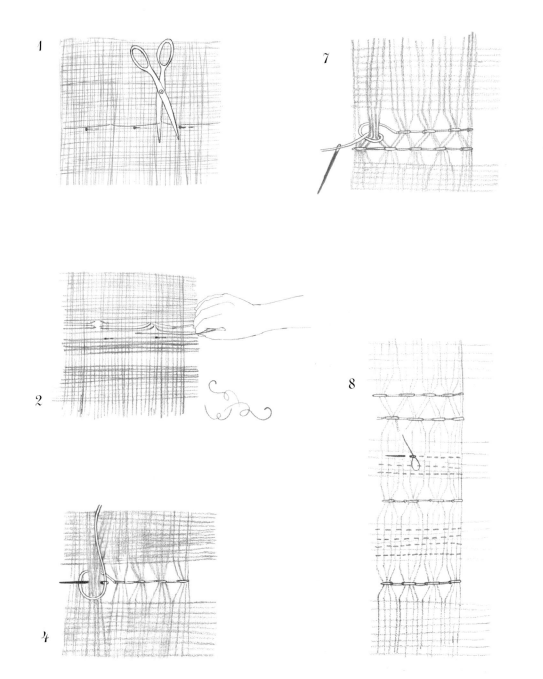

Drawn-Threadwork Runner

This kind of embroidery would normally be done as white on white and would use a much finer fabric. While white-on-white drawn threadwork is quite beautiful, it is also painstakingly slow to do. For beginners, therefore, the loose weave of the hessian used here provides an accessible introduction to this kind of embroidery (see photographs overleaf).

(see photographs overleaf)

INSTRUCTIONS

1. Cut a piece of hessian measuring 50 x 120cm (20 x 48in), ensuring that the fabric is cut straight and in line with the weave. Measure 3cm (1¼in) in from the raw edge and draw a line around all four sides with the dressmaker's chalk. Then machine-stitch along the chalked line in running stitch using black thread.

2. To make the fringe, carefully cut the warp threads (the vertical threads as the fabric was woven) on the longest sides of the runner and pull them out one by one until you reach the line of stitching. Repeat for the short edges, pulling out the weft threads (the horizontal threads as the fabric was woven) in the same way.

3. Measure 10cm (4in) in from the edge of the fringing and, using a ruler and dressmaker's chalk, draw a line around all four sides making sure that the lines are straight and running along either a warp or a weft thread (this will make it much easier to remove threads). Then draw another set of lines 3cm (1in) in from the lines you have just drawn.

4. To remove threads from within these parallel lines, start with the shorter ends of the rectangle. Using the chalk lines as a guide, carefully cut the weft threads and pull out the threads one by one. You may have to unweave the thread if the fabric is very stiff. Remove the warp threads from the long sides of the rectangle using the same technique.

5. Using cream embroidery thread, start by binding the two raw edges of each corner square with closely worked short-stemmed blanket stitch (see pages 22–3).

6. Turn the fabric over so you are working with the wrong side facing and work spoke stitch along the remaining edges of the pulled-thread frame. Working from left to right, secure the thread and then pass the needle over and around the three adjacent threads. Insert the needle through the edge of the fabric just next to the bundle of threads you have caught up, as shown, and pull tight to secure the stitch (see page 79 for more details). Repeat this process until all the edges are stitched in this way and the threads are sewn into bundles of three.

7. Overcast stitch, where embroidery thread is tightly wrapped around the length of an individual bundle, is used to create the bars. First count the bundles of threads in each border and calculate the intervals for the overcast bars. Here, they have been worked on every tenth bundle of thread.

MATERIALS

Black hessian

Scissors

Steel ruler

Dressmaker's chalk

Sewing machine

Black sewing thread

Cream embroidery thread

Needle

8. To make the overcast bars, work with the right side uppermost and use three strands of embroidery thread. Hold the end of the thread along the length of the bundle to be overcast so that it lies a third of the way down from the top and, starting at the top, pass the needle under and around the bundle from right to left.

9. Work down the length of the bundle, passing the needle from right to left under and around the bundle until it is completely covered. To secure the thread, slide the needle under four or five of the coils on the reverse side of the fabric and cut the thread.

TIP After you have made the first two or three coils on an overcast bar, pull taut the end of the embroidery thread lying along the bundle to tighten the coils. You can use the tip of the needle to push the coils up so that they lie next to one another without any gaps.

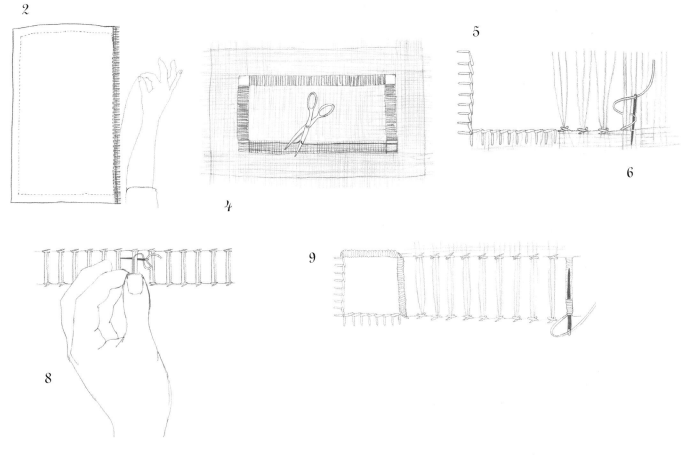

Templates

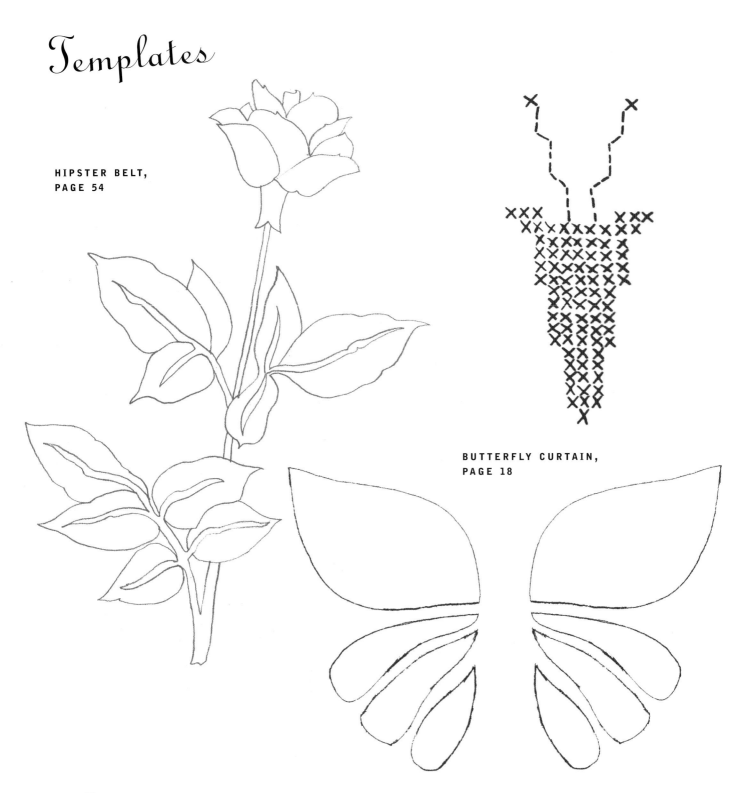

**HIPSTER BELT,
PAGE 54**

**BUTTERFLY CURTAIN,
PAGE 18**

LAVENDER SACHET,
PAGE 12

DAISY-CHAIN SCARF,
PAGE 44

FLORAL SKIRT,
PAGE 58

Addresses

ABBOTT & BOYD

1/22 Chelsea Harbour Design Centre,
London, SW10 0XE
020 7351 9985
Designer furnishing fabrics for
upholstery, curtains, drapes, cushions
and pillows

ANDREW MARTIN

200 Walton Street, London, SW3 2LJ
020 7225 5100
www.andrewmartin.co.uk
Furnishing fabrics and trimmings

ANNA FRENCH

343 Kings Road, London, SW3 5ES
020 7351 1126
www.annafrench.co.uk
Range of modern and traditional
furnishing fabrics, lace and accessories

ANTIQUE CRAFTS

276 West Wycombe Road,
High Wycombe, Bucks, HP12 4AB
01494 447514
www.antiquecrafts.co.uk
Mail-order supplier of craft products,
offering a huge range of buttons, lace,
beads, embellishments and trimmings

BARNYARNS

Canal Wharf, Bondgate Green,
Ripon, North Yorkshire, HG4 1BR
0870 870 8586
www.barnyarns.com
Extensive sewing and embroidery
mail-order supplies

THE BEAD SHOP

21a Tower Street,
London, WC2H 9NS
020 7240 0931

www.beadworks.co.uk
All types of beads, including
semi-precious stones

THE BERWICK STREET CLOTH SHOP

14 Berwick Street, London, W1F 0PP
020 7287 2881
Comprehensive range of fabrics
from wool to silk

BOGOD MACHINE COMPANY

Bogod House, 50–2 Great Sutton
Street, London, EC1V 0DJ
020 7253 1198
For sewing machines, overlockers
and accessories

THE BUTTON QUEEN

19 Marylebone Lane,
London, W1V 2NF
020 7935 1505
www.thebuttonqueen.co.uk
Every type of button you can
imagine and more!

CATH KIDSTON

51 Marylebone High Street,
London, W1U 5HW
020 7935 6555
Mail order: 020 7229 8000
www.cathkidston.co.uk
Furnishing fabrics and oilcloths

COATS CRAFTS

PO Box 22, Lingfield Point,
McMullen Road, Darlington,
Co. Durham, DL1 1YQ
01325 394237
www.coatscrafts.co.uk
For machine embroidery and
sewing threads

CRAFT DEPOT

Somerton Business Park,
Somerton, Somerset, TA11 6SB
01458 274727
www.craftdepot.co.uk
Mail-order craft supplies

CRAFTMISTRESS

66 Green Lane, Ockbrook,
Derby, DE27 3SE
01332 678945
www.craftmistress.co.uk
Embroidery and sewing products

CRAFTY RIBBONS

3 Beechwood Clump Farm,
Tin Pot Lane, Blandford,
Dorset, DT11 7TD
01258 455889
www.craftyribbons.com
Ribbon emporium

DESIGNERS GUILD

267 & 277 Kings Road,
London, SW3 5EN
020 7351 5775
www.designersguild.com
Modern interiors textiles,
upholstery and soft furnishings

G J BEADS

Court Arcade, The Wharf,
St Ives, Cornwall, TR26 1LG
01736 793886
www.gjbeads.co.uk
Mail-order beading supplies

HOBBY CRAFT

Forbury Retail Park, Off Kenavon
Drive, Reading, Berkshire, RG1 3HS
0118 902 8600
For store locations call:

0800 027 2387
www.hobbycraft.co.uk
Craft materials and equipment

HOME CRAFTS DIRECT

0116 269 7733
www.homecraftsdirect.co.uk
Mail-order craft materials

IAN MANKIN

109 Regents Park Road,
London, NW1 8UR
020 7722 0997
Mail order: 020 7722 0997
Includes good range of linen, cottons,
tickings, stripes and checks

JENNIFER GAIL THREADS

Studio, 1–3 Poole Hill,
Bournemouth, Dorset, BH2 5PW
01202 314144
www.jgthreads.com
Extensive range of space-dyed threads
and fabrics for embroidery, patchwork
and all textile art or craft

JOHN LEWIS

278–306 Oxford Street,
London, W1A 1EX
020 7629 7711
www.johnlewis.com
Fashion and furnishing fabric
department and good haberdashery.
Check the website for store locations

LAURA ASHLEY

256–8 Regent Street,
London, W1L 5DA
020 7437 9760
For a catalogue call: 08712 302301
www.lauraashley.com
Varied range of soft-furnishing fabrics

LIBERTY

Regent Street, London, W1B 5AH
020 7734 1234
www.liberty.co.uk
Dress and furnishing fabric
departments, plus embroidery
threads and trimmings

MALABAR

31–3 The South Bank
Business Centre, Ponton Road,
London, SW8 5BL
020 7501 4200
www.malabar.co.uk
Furnishing fabrics available
worldwide through interior
designers and retail outlets

OSBORNE & LITTLE

304 Kings Road, London, SW3 5UH
020 7352 1456
www.osborneandlittle.com
Leading designer of traditional
furnishing fabrics and wallpapers

PONGEES

28–30 Hoxton Square,
London, N1 6NN
020 7739 9130
www.pongees.co.uk
Specialize in silk and offer a huge
range; mail-order service available

RAINBOW MAIL ORDER SILKS

6 Wheelers Yard, High Street,
Great Missenden, Buckinghamshire,
HP16 0AL
01494 862111
www.rainbowsilks.co.uk
Stockists and mail-order suppliers
of a huge range of products for
embroidery and textile art and crafts,

including dyes, silks, velvets, paints
and dissolvable fabrics

ROWAN YARNS

Green Mill Lane, Holmfirth,
West Yorkshire, HD9 2DX
01484 681881
www.knitrowan.com
Comprehensive range of beautiful
natural yarns

**SHOREHAM KNITTING
& NEEDLECRAFT**

19 East Street, Shoreham-by-Sea,
West Sussex, BN43 5ZE
01273 461029
www.englishyarns.co.uk
Online yarn and thread store

**THE VOIRREY EMBROIDERY
CENTRE**

Brimstage Hall, Brimstage,
Wirral, CH63 6JA
0151 3423514
www.voirrey.com
Textile, needlework and knitting
stockists and mail-order suppliers

V V ROULEAUX

6 Marylebone High Street,
London, W1M 3PB
020 7224 5179
Huge range of trimmings in every
imaginable fabric and colourway

WHALEYS

Harris Court, Great Horton,
Bradford, West Yorkshire, BD7 4EQ
01274 576718
www.whaleys-bradford.ltd.uk
Stock includes utility fabrics, silks,
linen and jutes

Index

Acknowledgments

This book would not have been possible without the hard work and efforts of the following people, so a big thank you to you all: Zia Mattocks, who kept it all together; Chris Tubbs, and his assistant Natasha Sturny, for all the lush pictures in this book; Art Directors, Jonathan Christie and Lucy Gowans, who was always jolly; Nicky Barneby for her beautiful design; editor Emma Clegg and illustrator Alice Tate.